NATIVE AMERICAN NATIONS

Navajo

F.A. BIRD

CONTENT CONSULTANT: KELSEY DAYLE JOHN, PHD

Checkerboard
Library

An Imprint of Abdo Publishing
abdobooks.com

ABDOBOOKS.COM

Published by Abdo Publishing, a division of ABDO, PO Box 398166, Minneapolis, Minnesota 55439.
Copyright © 2022 by Abdo Consulting Group, Inc. International copyrights reserved in all countries.
No part of this book may be reproduced in any form without written permission from the publisher.
Checkerboard Library™ is a trademark and logo of Abdo Publishing.

Printed in the United States of America, North Mankato, Minnesota
102021
012022

 THIS BOOK CONTAINS RECYCLED MATERIALS

Design and Production: Mighty Media, Inc.
Editor: Liz Salzmann
Cover Photograph: Ruslan Kalnitsky/Shutterstock Images
Interior Photographs: Ad_hominem/Shutterstock Images, p. 7; Bhammond/Alamy Photo, p. 23; Billy
    McDonald/Shutterstock Images, p. 11; Chuck Coker/Flickr, p. 21; CoolPhotography/iStockphoto, p. 25;
    corumov/Shutterstock Images, p. 5; grandriver/iStockphoto, pp. 13, 15, 17; Hoptocopter/iStockphoto,
    p. 19; Malachi Jacobs/Shutterstock Images, p. 9; Smithsonian Institute's Anthropological Archives/
    Wikimedia Commons, p. 27; US Marine Corps/National Archives, p. 29

Library of Congress Control Number: 2021943041

Publisher's Cataloging-in-Publication Data
Names: Bird, F.A., author.
Title: Navajo / by F.A. Bird
Description: Minneapolis, Minnesota : Abdo Publishing, 2022 | Series: Native American nations | Includes
    online resources and index.
Identifiers: ISBN 9781532197208 (lib. bdg.) | ISBN 9781098219338 (ebook)
Subjects: LCSH: Navajo Indians--Juvenile literature. | Indians of North America--Juvenile literature. |
    Indigenous peoples--Social life and customs--Juvenile literature. | Cultural anthropology--Juvenile
    literature.
Classification: DDC 973.0497--dc23

Contents

CHAPTER 1

Homelands

Over one thousand years ago, the Navajo and their Apache relatives lived in northern Canada and Alaska. Over time, they moved south.

Some traveled east of the Rocky Mountains. Some went through present-day Nevada and Utah. Most eventually arrived in the deserts of northern New Mexico and Arizona. The Navajo call themselves *Diné*. It means "the people."

Monument Valley Tribal Park is part of the Navajo Nation. It sits on the border of Arizona and Utah.

CHAPTER 2

Society

The Navajo lived in **clan** groups of a few related families. The society is matrilineal. This means **ancestry** and kinship is traced through the mothers. Navajo clans were spread over a wide area. They lived among neighboring tribes such as the Pueblo.

The Navajo were warriors and **hunter-gatherers**. The Pueblo taught the Navajo how to grow corn, melons, beans, and squash. The Navajo also raised sheep and other livestock.

The Navajo wove rugs and made beautiful jewelry. They often used **turquoise** and other stones they considered sacred.

THE NAVAJO HOMELANDS

CHAPTER 3

Homes

Traditional Navajo family homes are called *hogans*. *Hogans* are made of logs and rocks. They are framed in a circle about 30 feet (9 m) wide. The frames are covered with mud. The mud keeps the *hogans* cool inside.

Each *hogan* has one door. The door faces east to greet the morning sun, which is sacred to the Navajo. A hole in the *hogan's* roof releases smoke from the fire inside. Some *hogans* also have several outside shade shelters.

A shade shelter has a roof of sticks and bushes. Four or six posts hold the roof up. It protects people, supplies, and tools from the sun and rain. The Navajo often fixed their breakfast in the shade shelters.

Today, Navajo people enjoy working outside weaving rugs. They also sit outside and talk.

Today, most Navajo *hogans* are used for special ceremonies rather than as homes.

CHAPTER 4

Food

Waking up early was very important to the Navajo. Breakfast was supposed to be ready by daybreak. Often it was **tortillas** and **mutton** stew. Roast mutton was another favorite food.

The main meals were often vegetable and potato stews. Sometimes the stews had lamb, sheep, or goat meat in them. They were served with tortillas.

Corn, wheat, and vegetables were grown in the family fields. Women and children often gathered prickly pears, peaches, and **piñon nuts**. The women also gathered herbs and spices. They used these to make teas.

Piñon nuts come from the piñon pine, which grows throughout the American Southwest.

CHAPTER 5

Clothing

Men and women usually made their own clothes. When the Navajo first came to the desert, they wore deerskin clothes. Later they made clothes out of cotton and wool. These materials were better for the hot climate. They kept people cooler than deerskin.

Women wore a dress called a *biil*. A *biil* was a blanket or large shawl. It had a slit in the middle. This allowed the head to slip through. The *biil* hung down past the knees. It was open on both sides. The *biil* was gathered around the waist with a belt.

Men wore a shorter blanket or shawl. It, too, was gathered at the waist with a belt. Men also wore pants of woven cloth or deerskin.

Many Navajo wear belts known as concho belts. These leather belts feature round silver pieces with decorative patterns.

CHAPTER 6

Crafts

Navajo women are known for weaving blankets and rugs. The women use **looms** for their weaving. They place different colored threads on the loom. These threads are woven into patterns that tell stories important to the Navajo people. As they work, the women often sing songs.

Navajo men first learned to make silver jewelry from Mexican jewelers in the 1850s. The Navajo create bracelets, necklaces, and belt buckles from silver dollars and **turquoise** stones.

Navajo blankets are often woven from brightly colored threads.

CHAPTER 7

Family

Each Navajo person is considered to have four **clans**. The first clan is their mother's. This means they take their mother's clan name. The other three clans are their father's clan and both of their grandfathers' clans. In this way, the Navajo trace their **ancestry**.

When someone wants to get married, they must choose someone with a different clan. Married people build their home near the bride's mother. Women make most of the important family decisions. They own the family's material possessions. Men respect women as the possessors of wealth.

Women owned all Navajo possessions, including livestock such as sheep.

CHAPTER 8

Children

Navajo children often grew up with many brothers, sisters, and cousins nearby. The older children guided the younger ones around the home and land as everyone worked.

Mothers, aunts, and grandmothers gave the children many tasks each day. Five- and six-year-olds carried water from the stream. Older children helped the **elders** cook and chop wood. Both boys and girls learned how to ride horses and work the sheep and cattle.

Young girls learned to weave by watching their mothers. They helped pick the wild plants that made different dyes. The dyes colored the thread made from sheep's wool.

A Navajo grandmother teaches her granddaughters how to weave.

CHAPTER 9

Medicine People

The Navajo saw illness as a disturbance in the universe. Medicine people used special healing ceremonies to restore order so the sick person would get well. A healing ceremony often included a sand painting. The medicine person arranged colored sand into sacred images and patterns. Sand paintings could be one to twenty feet (0.3 to 6 m) across. They could take many hours to finish.

During a healing ceremony, the sick person sat on the sand painting. The medicine person sang songs of healing. This was to encourage the good energy in the sand painting to heal the person and draw the illness into the painting. When the healing ceremony was over, the sand painting was destroyed.

Singing is an important part of many Navajo ceremonies. Navajo singers spend many years learning the sacred songs.

A Navajo medicine man gathers wild sage. This plant is used in many Navajo medicines and ceremonies.

CHAPTER 10

War

The Navajo were fierce warriors. When they first came to the desert, they fought the Pueblo, Ute, and Comanche for land. They also fought to protect their lands from Spanish, Mexican, and American colonizers during the 1800s.

During the Navajo War of 1863 to 1866, the US government forced the Navajo from their homelands. The Navajo people were forced to march to Fort Sumner in eastern New Mexico. This march is known as the Long Walk.

Many **elders** and young children died on the march and at Fort Sumner. Some were too weak to make the journey. Others became ill or starved to death.

In 1868, the Navajo signed a treaty with the US government. They negotiated with the government so they could return to their homelands.

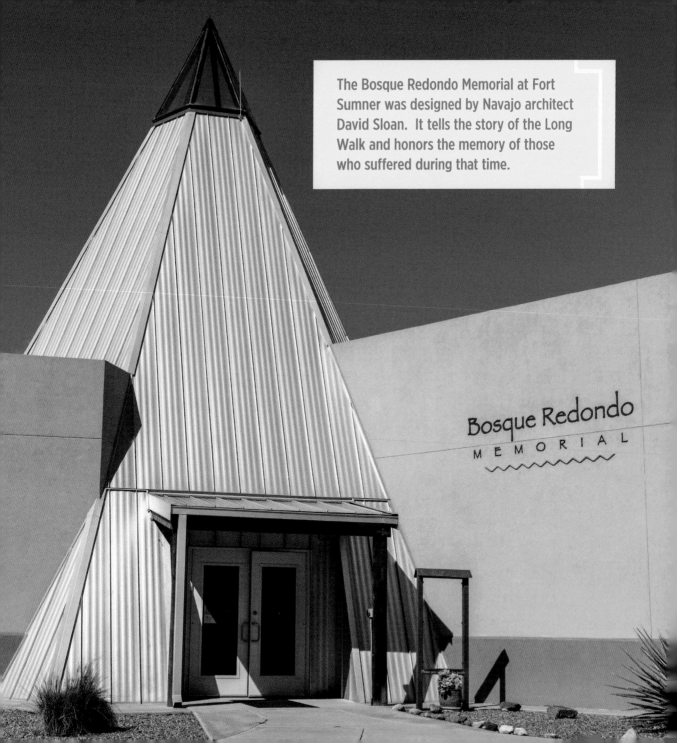

The Bosque Redondo Memorial at Fort Sumner was designed by Navajo architect David Sloan. It tells the story of the Long Walk and honors the memory of those who suffered during that time.

Bosque Redondo
MEMORIAL

CHAPTER 11

Contact with Europeans

In 1582, Spanish explorer Antonio de Espejo led his troops into the Navajo homelands from Mexico. It was the first time the Navajo had seen Europeans.

The Spanish described the Navajo as peaceful. The Navajo brought the explorers **tortillas** when they met. However, the Spanish still settled on Navajo land and captured Navajo people to serve as slaves. This led to many years of conflict as the Navajo tried to protect their lands and people.

The Spanish brought domestic animals such as horses, sheep, and goats to North America. These animals became an important part of life for the Navajo and other Native peoples.

CHAPTER 12

Barboncito

Two years after the Long Walk, the US government
wanted the Navajo to move again. The government
planned to move the Navajo to a **reservation** in Oklahoma.
Barboncito, one of the first Navajo leaders, negotiated
with the government officials.

Barboncito signed a treaty between the Navajo and the
United States on June 1, 1868. It established the original
Navajo Reservation in the Chuska Mountains of Arizona.
The treaty promised the Navajo they could live on their
homelands. Barboncito died three years later.

Barboncito

CHAPTER 13

The Navajo Today

In 1923, the Navajo tribal government was founded. The tribal government has legislative, executive, and judicial branches. The Navajo sell oil and mineral deposits from their lands. This is one way the tribal government raises money.

During **World War II**, Navajo Code Talkers helped the US military pass important messages. The Navajo language was unlike European languages. This made it perfect for sending coded messages.

Today, the Navajo Nation is the largest Native American tribe in the United States. More than 200,000 people live in the Navajo Nation, which stretches through northern Arizona, Utah, and New Mexico. Many Navajo people have made important contributions to science, art, government, and business.

About 400 Navajo Code Talkers served during World War II. Their work led to many US victories during the war.

Glossary

ancestry—a line of descent.

clan—an extended family sharing a common ancestor.

elder—a person having authority because of age or experience.

hunter-gatherers—people who feed themselves solely by hunting and gathering food. Hunter-gatherers do not grow crops.

loom—a wooden frame that is used to weave cloth or blankets from thread.

mutton—the meat of an older sheep.

piñon nuts—seeds that grow on piñons, or pine trees.

reservation—a piece of land set aside by the government for Native Americans to live on.

tortilla—a corn pancake used by many Native American tribes.

turquoise—a clear blue or greenish-blue precious stone used in jewelry.

World War II—from 1939 to 1945, fought in Europe, Asia, and Africa. Great Britain, France, the United States, the Soviet Union, and their allies were on one side. Germany, Italy, Japan, and their allies were on the other side.

ONLINE RESOURCES

Booklinks
NONFICTION NETWORK
FREE! ONLINE NONFICTION RESOURCES

To learn more about the Navajo, please visit **abdobooklinks.com** or scan this QR code. These links are routinely monitored and updated to provide the most current information available.

Index